RESCUE THE DEAD

Drawing by Rose Graubart

RESCUE

THE

DEAD

Poems by DAVID IGNATOW

Many of these poems have previously appeared elsewhere. For permission to reprint and for assigning copyrights to him, the author is grateful to the editors and publishers of the following:

Athanor, Choice, December, Poetry, Floating World, Frostbite, Grist, IT, kayak, The Nation, The New York Times, North American Review, Perspective, The Poetry Bag, Poganoggan, Quarterly Review of Literature, The Sixties, Some/Thing, and Tennessee Poetry Journal.

"Anew" (there titled "Dante Forgot") and the final stanza of "Six Movements on a Theme" (there titled "The Massage") were first printed in Elizabeth.

"Sediment" appeared originally in The New Yorker.

"All Quiet", "For Nobody Else", "The Hope", "On the Death of Churchill," and "Rescue the Dead" were first published in Poetry.

The author thanks the John Simon Guggenheim Memorial Foundation for a year of writing time during which more than a few of these poems were made.

WESLEYAN UNIVERSITY PRESS

Middletown, Connecticut

Library of Congress Catalog Card Number: 68–16005
Manufactured in the United States of America
First edition

Many of these poems have previously appeared elsewhere. For permission
to reprint and for assigning copyrights to him, the author is grateful to the
editors and publishers of the following:
*Athanor, Choice, December, Epoch, Floating World, Frostbite, Grist, IT,
kayak, The Nation, The New York Times, North American Review,
Perspective, The Poetry Bag, Pogamoggan, Quarterly Review of Literature,
The Sixties, Some/Thing,* and *Tennessee Poetry Journal.*
"Anew" (there titled "Dante Forgot") and the final stanza of "Six Move-
ments on a Theme" (there titled "The Message") were first printed in
Elizabeth.
"Sediment" appeared originally in *The New Yorker.*
"All Quiet," "For Nobody Else," "The Hope," "On the Death of Chur-
chill," and "Rescue the Dead" were first published in *Poetry.*
The author thanks the John Simon Guggenheim Memorial Foundation for
a year of writing time during which more than a few of these poems were
made.

Library of Congress Catalog Card Number: 68–16005
Manufactured in the United States of America
First edition

I feel along the edges of life
for a way
that will lead to open land.

Contents

RESCUE THE DEAD

RESCUE THE DEAD

Prologue

Mine was the life planned to go wrong
and to make havoc among the living.
From me you know what is monstrous
about being alive
and to forgive myself
and go on eating.
I must act like you.

I get up sick inside,
I lie down unlearnt
and in my sleep
hear a wishful tide
cleaning, cleaning.

I was born of parents who had small comfort
for one another. When they met
it was to recognize their need for contrast
and it turned out
they rubbed each other the wrong way.

So when you find out your father
spends his days looking at lewd photos,
you yourself feel so happy and relieved.
Your stomach quakes, your head thick
with whispers, your legs trembling.

11

The Boss

who hoarded among the monthly bank statements
nude photos,
the drawer locked,
the key in his pocket,
still could complain
of the stupidity of his help—
their incompetency,
their secretiveness;
he could sense it
in their guarded snickers
when he criticized;
who could walk the shop
in possession as he walked,
stoop-shouldered, careless
how he went, sagging;
it was his shop
and his machinery
and his steel cabinet
where the photos lay.

In Absentia

You sunken-cheeked lover of yourself,
you wronged self-lover, sad-eyed murderer
of another person's love of you:
coffin builder, hammer and nail wielder,
you laugh of disrespect
from where you hate yourself.
I am so bitter.
Don't you know better than to make me say
what should be struggled with and tempered,
the raw words? I am the sick one.

Your embittered boasting
more revealing than a knife
and even more hurtful.
No one can get at it to restrain you,
no one but you and you refuse,
cutting both ways.

I put this on the page to make you listen.
I believe in telepathy, I believe you know
what I am writing and I believe you are answering
with stubbornness and abuse and self-righteousness,
"I am the boss!" Do you not see I am lost
because you are? This is your illness.

I want you dead of guilt and shame.
Give me this last chance to be ashamed
of my raging and sin against you.

I never thought your harsh voice would be silenced,
your contracted, vicious face relaxed and calm,
the big nose standing out magisterially
and the once small, sharp, puckered mouth
lengthened into a soft, sad curve,
reminding me of your mother's photograph.
I kissed your cold forehead with my fingertips
first touched to my lips in farewell,
and as I lingered to study your face
the lid was slammed down by attendants
to get them on with their job. Later
I wept, and my wife too was impatient with me,
knowing you well. Nevertheless, I wept.
You gave me smiles and made me work
at your machines. It was you taught me
the necessity for freedom.
I am going to sell your shop,
you to be remembered in my lines.

There were no hidden motives to his life,
he is remembered for his meanness.
Beyond that we may look into the sky
and lose ourselves in the blue air.

Reason with me,
I'll believe in reason
though my father is dead,
and when I die
remember of me
I sought for a reason.

In the mirror the face I see
before me is my father's face,
as if I were thinking his thoughts
about me, in love
and disapproval.
I turn my face away.

Forgive me, father,
as I have forgiven you
my sins.

Nourish the Crops

I examine the sun for my life's goodness.
warmed on body, face and hands. Panic
seizes me. I may be acting a part,
self-consciously the mendicant.
I gasp for air through a chest gripped
in fear of my life. It is death for me
who am still guilty at the very heart,
still the one who needs forgiveness,
to whom this finding of the sun is a ruse
to forget. True as I breathe, I tell myself.
It is just as I say. Back to this understanding
of myself, my breathing becomes normal.
Guilty in the sun. My peace now is truthful,
I am truthfully at peace. Oh sun,
your kindness is a mystery to me.
How dark I am to myself. How cold I am to myself.
How close to death I bring myself.
Because I see you shine on me, I am amazed
at a loss about myself. I stop to reconsider
my purpose. Whose death am I seeking?
I feel myself inconsequential in your warmth
as it descends on me and on birds, flowers
and beasts. You give us life, no matter.
I feel humiliated in my self-importance.
My wish to die in retribution for my sins
is laughable. I die in any case like a flower
or bee or dog. Should I live then as you do
in brightness and warmth, without question?
Because I am product of you to whom all life
is equal. Do I not sin against you
by staying dark to myself? You who have given

the tiger and the snake life
and nourish the crops?

Slowly I move over the field,
one tired foot ahead of the other,
feeling through my soles
the rise and fall of the land.

The Moon

I walk beneath it, seeing a stranger
look down on my familiar state. I walk,
and it does not know where or for what
reason on the black surface of the earth.
I hurry, it is late. I disappear
into the dark shadow of a building,
running, and ask of the moon
what does it expect to discover,
what does it do in the sky,
staring down on the intimate
despairing actions of a man?

Self-Employed

(For Harvey Shapiro)

I stand and listen, head bowed,
to my inner complaint.
Persons passing by think
I am searching for a lost coin.
You're fired, I yell inside
after an especially bad episode.
I'm letting you go without notice
or terminal pay. You just lost
another chance to make good.
But then I watch myself standing at the exit,
depressed and about to leave,
and wave myself back in wearily,
for who else could I get in my place
to do the job in dark, airless conditions?

The Exchange

(For David)

You tell me how helpless you are to leave.
I listen, detached as you prefer me.
I hear screams from the building
across the grass, and laughter.
I scan your face as calm as mine.
We continue to sit under a shady tree.

I blotted him out with a drop of ink.
I absorbed him in my blotter.
Now when I look I find him
under a scratched-out word
under the influence of the x mark,
eyes lowered, smiling,
finding in himself that pleasure
that was crossed out for him,
his face calm and good.
He has his dream and will not raise
his eyes to give it up.

I stretch out a hand, a warding off of evil,
and it is grasped limply as you smile,
your eyes still averted. We get up
from the grass and go for coffee
at the Exchange.

Envoi

Strange judgment upon me:
I once said to my father,
You are not my father,
and I meant Karl Marx, Lenin, Whitman.
Today I have a son
to whom I am tempted to say,
You are not my son,
in the same passionate vindication
of myself.

Nice Guy

I had a friend and he died. Me.
I forgot to mourn him that busy day
earning a living. I heard a click
telling me his eyes had closed
for the last time inside me,
and I turned away, not of my own volition,
but getting an offer of a job
I answered politely, saying yes,
his death unfortunate at midday
during business. I apologized
but had no one to apologize to,
buried without me at work.
I mourn him now at leisure on the couch
after the day. He was a good guy,
he meant well, only he had lost his teeth
and had to swallow whole.
He died of too much.

The Bagel

I stopped to pick up the bagel
rolling away in the wind,
annoyed with myself
for having dropped it
as it were a portent.
Faster and faster it rolled,
with me running after it
bent low, gritting my teeth,
and I found myself doubled over
and rolling down the street
head over heels, one complete somersault
after another like a bagel
and strangely happy with myself.

Rescue the Dead

Finally, to forgo love is to kiss a leaf,
is to let rain fall nakedly upon your head,
is to respect fire,
is to study man's eyes and his gestures
as he talks,
is to set bread upon the table
and a knife discreetly by,
is to pass through crowds
like a crowd of oneself.
Not to love is to live.

To love is to be led away
into a forest where the secret grave
is dug, singing, praising darkness
under the trees.

To live is to sign your name,
is to ignore the dead,
is to carry a wallet
and shake hands.

To love is to be a fish.
My boat wallows in the sea.
You who are free,
rescue the dead.

A Suite for Marriage

You keep eating and raising a family
in an orderly, calm fashion
for the sake of the child,
but behind you at your heels
in a humble mass
lies a figure.

Do you own me?
I sense it in your nervous
irritated talk, as for someone
who has become a burden—
when what is possessed
becomes equally demanding
for being possessed.

I am not sure that you wish me to live.
I am not sure that I can.
We circle each other
with the taut courtesy
of two respectful opponents.
Difficult to say what next,
this could be all,
to confront each other
in suspense.

Your eyes are so cold-looking,
rejecting me silently
as I talk in low, cultured tones
to convince you
of my superiority.

So what shall they make of their daughter
who knows nothing of their unhappiness
with each other? She stands between them
like a light of many colors, turning
and dancing.

My daughter, I cry to you from my solitude.
I play the yea-sayer, most bitter,
to spare you with deeds I know can win
good from evil, my despair
a blessing for your life.

Notes for a Lecture

I will teach you to become American, my students:
take a turn at being enigmatic, to yourselves especially.
You work at a job and write poetry at night.
You write about working. Married,
you write about love.

I speak of kisses and mean quarrels,
the kiss brings the quarrel to mind,
of differences for their own sakes.

Did I ever think, going to bed,
a woman beside me would be no more uplifting
than a five-dollar raise? Since then
I've been uplifted in bed a hundred times
and but once raised in pay,
and that once has not been forgotten.

Take a broken whiskey bottle,
set it on top of your head
and dance. You have a costume,
you have meaning.

Love in a Zoo

What I offer she strips
and throws its peelings to the ground,
swallows the bulk in one gulp
and loses me in her stomach,
swinging back and forth by the tail
from a branch. Say to the monkey,
I need you, pat my cheek, kiss my brow.
Tell me it's wonderful to be given
a banana from my hands. Say
that you love me more each day
and do not know how you can survive
without me in the zoo. Say,
Let us make a home together.
Then I will feed you bananas all day
and little monkeys will spring up between us
secure and warm. Monkey, monkey
sends me home, scratching its buttocks
and picking fleas.

Sediment

You are such a well-rounded sponge
from head to foot
that I have made myself a lake for you
not to see you shrivel up
and I have surrounded you with trees
and a distant view of a mountain,
calm sky above.
No rain comes while you and I float together,
your reflection in me, and then slowly
you settle down, filled.
I think you are going to drown
and I will go dry, utterly absorbed in you,
my mud and rock showing. I worry about us,
you swollen and out of shape
and I tasting of sediment.

For Your Fear

Love me and I'll think about it
and perhaps love you,
if it goes with the moment
or in despite of that pose as lover
to find the truth of what to love.
Hate me for that matter
for being so plain
and I will have to think
and keep open between us lines
which might someday carry messages
when it's with you as with me.
Love me for my desperation
that I may love you for your fear.

The Room

There's a door to my name
shutting me in, with a seat
at a table behind the wall
where I suck of the lemon seed.
Farther in is the bed
I have made of the fallen hairs
of my love, naked, her head dry.
I speak of the making of charts
and prescriptions and matches
that light tunnels
under the sea.

A chair, a table, a leg of a chair—
I hold these with my eyes to keep from falling,
my thoughts holding to these shapes,
my breathing of them that make my body
mine through the working of my eyes.
All else is silence and falling.

In the dark
I hear wings beating
and move my arms around
and above
to touch.
My arms go up and down
and around
as I circle the room.

Ritual One

As I enter the theatre the play is going on.
I hear the father say to the son on stage,
You've taken the motor apart.
The son replies, The roof is leaking.
The father retorts, The tire is flat.
Tiptoeing down the aisle, I find my seat,
edge my way in across a dozen kneecaps
as I tremble for my sanity.
I have heard doomed voices calling on god the electrode.
Sure enough, as I start to sit
a scream rises from beneath me.
It is one of the players.
If I come down, I'll break his neck,
caught between the seat and the backrest.
Now the audience and the players on stage,
their heads turned towards me, are waiting
for the sound of the break. Must I?
Those in my aisle nod slowly, reading my mind,
their eyes fixed on me, and I understand
that each has done the same.
Must I kill this man as the price of my admission
to this play? His screams continue loud and long.
I am at a loss as to what to do,
I panic, I freeze.

My training has been to eat the flesh of pig.
I might even have been able to slit a throat.

As a child I witnessed the dead chickens
over a barrel of sawdust absorbing their blood.
I then brought them in a bag to my father
who sold them across his counter. Liking him,
I learned to like people and enjoy their company too,
which of course brought me to this play.
But how angry I become.
Now everybody is shouting at me to sit down,
sit down or I'll be thrown out.
The father and son have stepped off stage
and come striding down the aisle side by side.
They reach me, grab me by the shoulder
and force me down. I scream, I scream,
as if to cover the sound of the neck breaking.

All through the play I scream
and am invited on stage to take a bow.
I lose my senses and kick the actors in the teeth.
There is more laughter
and the actors acknowledge my performance with a bow.
How should I understand this?
Is it to say that if I machine-gun the theatre
from left to right they will respond with applause
that would only gradually diminish with each death?
I wonder then whether logically I should kill myself
too out of admiration. A question indeed,
as I return to my seat and observe a new act
of children playfully aiming their kicks
at each other's groins.

Ritual Two

The kids yell and paint their bodies
black and brown, their eyes bulging.
As they brush, they dance, weaving
contorted shapes. They drive each other
to the wall, to the floor, to the bed,
to the john, yelling, "Nothing!"
Now they race around in a circle,
pounding their bellies, and laughter
rises from among them. They begin
to take the stage apart on which they stand,
ripping, kicking and pounding.
I show them my palm,
the cavity of my mouth down to my larynx
and then as I begin my own dance—
it ends when I die—they lock hands
and circle around me, very glad, very comforted
for the circle shall be empty of me
and they, falling through the stage, will yell,
"Nothing!"
            I remove hat, coat, shoes, socks, pants
and undershirt. I make motions to the ceiling
to come down and make motions to the floor to open.
I pretend to write a check for all my money
and hand it around. Each refuses to take it
and continues to dance. I give the check
to a hand that reaches from the ceiling,
as the kids chant, "Nothing, Nothing!"

I pretend to hold a child by the hand
and walk as though strolling up a street
with him and stoop to listen to this child
and talk to him, when suddenly I act

as if shot, slowly falling to the ground,
kissing the child goodby with my fingertips,
but I spring up and pretend to be the child,
lost, abandoned, bewildered, wanting to die,
crouching as the circle keeps chanting,
"Nothing, Nothing!"
I then rise slowly to my full height,
having grown up through my agony.
I throw my head back proudly
and join hands with others as they dance,
chanting their theme. We converge in the center,
bang against each other, scream and scatter.

Ritual Three

In England, the slow methodical torture of two children
was recorded on tape by the murderers.

1

It's quiet for me, now that I have buried the child.
I am resting, rid of a menace to my peace,
since I am not here for long either.
What she said was that she wanted to go back
to her mother, so help her God, and I believed her,
and they did too who cut her slowly into flesh,
but it was another mother they had in mind.
Let me rest, let me rest from their mistakes.
They were human like myself, somehow
gone in a direction to a depth I've never known.
I am not thinking,
I am contemptuous of thought.
I growl in my depths, I find blood flowing
across my tongue and enjoy its taste.
Call me man, I don't care.
I am content with myself,
I have a brain that gives me the pleasure.
Come here and I will tear you to pieces,
it'll be catch as catch can
but I can throw you who are weakened with the horror
of what I say, so surrender peacefully
and let me take my first bite directly above your heart.
I am a man, your life lost in feeling,
I never knew what mercy meant,
I am free.

2

Child gone to a calm grave,
I want to be a crocodile,
opening the two blades of my mouth.
I'll slide through swamp, taking in small fish and flies.
I will not run a knife across the skin
or cut off a nose or tear off the genitals,
as screams fade in exhaustion.
Nobody could force me, as I threaten with my jaws,
safe for a moment as I dream I am sane, purposeful
and on my course, dreaming that we no longer should trouble
to live as human beings, that we should discuss this,
putting aside our wives and children,
for to live is to act in terms of death.

The Open Boat

With no place to lay my head
beside a friend
who could give peace,
none to guard my door
nor still my house,
I am five miles out: the sea
flexes its muscles
and I have gulls for companions
overhead—veering off,
afraid, afraid
of a human.

A Dialogue

I now will throw myself down
from a great height
to express sorrow.
Step aside, please.
I said please step aside
and permit me access
to the building's edge.
How is this, restrained,
encircled by arms,
in front of me a crowd?
I cannot be detained in this manner.
Hear me, I speak with normal emotion.
Release me,
I would express sorrow in its pure form.
I am insane, you say
and will send me away—
and I will go
and die there
in sorrow.

From a Dream

I'm on a stair going down.
I must get to a landing
where I can order food
and relax with a newspaper.
I should retrace my steps to be sure,
but the stairs above disappear into clouds.
But down is where I want to go,
these stairs were built to lead somewhere
and I would find out.
As I keep walking,
ever more slowly,
I leave notes such as this on the steps.
There must be an end to them
and I will get to it,
just as did the builders,
if only I were sure now
that these stairs were built
by human hands.

The Derelict

I'm going to be dead a long time,
says an old man, adjusting his trousers
in the public toilet. They hang down
below his buttocks, with legs spread apart,
he is tucking in his long underwear.
"I'll be dead a long time."

Lying curled up on the ground
against the wall, he is
a grey-haired foetus
which has given up
and returned to its mother.
Round and round she whirls
in space.

East Bronx

In the street two children sharpen
knives against the curb.
Parents leaning out the window
above gaze and think and smoke
and duck back into the house
to sit on the toilet seat
with locked door to read
of the happiness of two tortoises
on an island in the Pacific—
always alone and always
the sun shining.

I See a Truck

I see a truck mowing down a parade,
people getting up after to follow,
dragging a leg. On a corner
a cop stands idly swinging his club,
the sidewalks jammed with mothers
and baby carriages. No one screams
or speaks. From the tail end
of the truck a priest and a rabbi intone
their prayers, a jazz band bringing up
the rear, surrounded by dancers and lovers.
A bell rings and a paymaster drives through,
his wagon filled with pay envelopes
he hands out, even to those lying dead
or fornicating on the ground.
It is a holiday called
"Working for a Living."

All Quiet

(For Robert Bly)
Written at the start of one of our bombing pauses
over North Vietnam

How come nobody is being bombed today?
I want to know, being a citizen
of this country and a family man.
You can't take my fate in your hands,
without informing me.
I can blow up a bomb or crush a skull—
whoever started this peace
without advising me
through a news leak
at which I could have voiced a protest,
running my whole family off a cliff.

An American Parable

Good boys are we to have retrieved
                            for its owner the ball
which first we dipped in liquid gold
                            with affection.
Now he keeps pitching it farther and farther,
curious, excited and alarmed,
nor can we understand,
since it is returned to him
each time heavier with gold
and less wieldy.

A Meditation on Violence

It is perfectly possible
                    like a boar
          swinging his tusk

                    It is he
caught upon a spear
                    bleeding
stretched out on the ground

                    We bow

On my birthday
they knocked out
two bridges
a fishing boat standing at anchor
and a forest
defoliated with a napalm bomb
on my fifty-first year

Saying "Peace"
is to keep the dogs down
who are straining to leap
savage and whining
out of our own mouths

Through an open window
facing the river
the wind blows this hot day
while I sprawl upon a bed,
my skin cooled. Would
that this were the fate of the world:

a stream of cool reason
flow serenely between hot shores
into which steaming heads
could dip themselves

But the children, I think, should not be blotted out,
as I sit listening to the rise and fall
of their pleasures, the sudden change
to bad temper quickly forgotten
by the shift to joy,
pleased with the world that lets them
shout and jump and play at tantrums
for this is freedom to understand
until they wander off to bed.
Shall I say their sounds are an intrusion
when they show the meaning to my life
is to celebrate, always to celebrate?
I listen as I would to rain falling
upon a field.

For Medgar Evers

They're afraid of me
because I remind them of the ground.
The harder they step on me
the closer I am pressed to earth,
and hard, hard they step,
growing more frightened
and vicious.

                Will I live?
They will lie in the earth
buried in me
and above them a tree will grow
for shade.

On the Death of Winston Churchill

Now should great men die
in turn one by one
to keep the mind solemn
and ordained,
the living attend in dark clothes
and with tender weariness
and crowds at television sets
and newsstands wait
as each man's death sustains a peace.
The great gone, the people
one by one
offer to die.

Christ

All men betray me
who betray myself to men
through goodness
taken as an offense to them.
I die of my joy in life
and go dwell with the dead
who are accepted
trodden on
as of the earth itself.

Soldier

In his hands the submachine gun is excited,
pouring its life out; he is detached,
searching for bodies. I am detached,
wondering whether to stuff and hang him
on my wall a trophy. From behind,
I could put a bullet through his head
and as he sinks dropping his gun,
rip off his clothes, slice him down the middle,
pull out his liver, heart, spleen,
the whole works from head to bowels,
his brain poked out through his nostrils
to keep his skull intact.
I'd leave his eyes in,
treat them chemically to last
for their lustrous quality.
I'd stuff with dried grass the cavities of his body
to achieve their natural proportions,
then glue him to the surface of a board
the length of his frame, hang him on the wall
in my study, the submachine gun stuck back
in his hands, his mouth straightened
in a killer's line, except
I lack his calculating way to do it,
and can only write this to say
in any case
he is finished.

In My Childhood

A yellow canary looked at me
sideways through its wired cage
and I said to my friend with me,
I want to hold this tiny bird.
But he began talking of his air gun
and I got the use of it
that day for one hour.

The Signal

How can I regret my life
when I find the blue-green traffic light
on the corner delightful against the red brick
of my house. It is when the signal turns red
that I lose interest. At night
I am content to watch the blue-green
come on again against the dark
and I do not torture myself
with my shortcomings.

Domestic Song

My lovely Rose who forgives me
by speaking of herself as I do
when I have turned her image into faults.
It is then she sweetly wars with me
by herself losing, asking
how can I live with one
who does not know enough
to stir leg or arm from harm
or foolish action. She is bent
upon my distraction, for which I do penance
by laughter and thereafter know
myself as one who cannot rule his judgment,
a drudge to his own faults,
seeking to enlighten others
that he may stay in his dark alone.
Of this she says nothing, but speaks
of herself in the negative, that I the more quickly
may myself forgive. I love her
for this beauty she would conjure up,
and when it is accomplished she will say,
That is fine, bit by bit.
She is my love for everyday
and darkness is the absence of her;
and so it is enough for any man
that he may do as much in this world
as to have a Rose for his woman.

An Allegory

I offer my back to the silken net
to keep it from falling to the ground—
the smooth part of me,
silk would catch on my nails,
the skein spread as far as I can see
across humped backs like mine.
Those straightening up
through a rip and looking about
say, "How everything shines."

The Pleasure

With broken tooth he clawed it,
with crooked finger held it,
and with naked eyes watched it
as he chewed, hair disheveled,
tie loose, shirt open, socks down—
a bum, greedy, therefore knowing.
How he chewed and how he swallowed
and wiped his lips with the back of his palm,
then spat blood of the raw-veined
brick-red lump meat; and went
looking for more down the side streets
of the market where the trash cans stank,
and came up with chunks greening
at the center and edges, but he chewed
and swallowed and dug for more,
a bum greedy, a bum alive,
a hungry one.

To Make Known

(For Zero Mostel)

I noticed you waddled
as you approached my desk with widening eyes.
You enquired about your mother's condition.
It was my job to tell you she was dead.
I had read of you, a great clown,
in off-Broadway productions.
I wanted to make known to you my admiration.
You were pathetic as the son of a dead woman.
A mother's tolerance of your faults was gone.
I meant to comfort you
from behind my hospital information desk.
I was just beginning to write my poems,
I had no prestige, except for a few boyhood friends,
tolerant, as they pulled ahead in money and place,
in chosen professions. Your response would have helped.
I finished notifying you of her death
and started to express my sympathy.
You said, Thank you, in the coldest way—
you a fat man, a comedian, source of joy and humour,
open to all weaknesses within,
to whom weakness was a gift.
What another side there was, as you turned away,
your mouth, eyes and cheeks overflowing their sources
in all directions.
Perhaps it was embarrassment—
you may have realized I recognized you.

No ordinary man, you who showed your faults to others.
I shrank within as you moved off.
I might have gotten up from behind my desk
to follow and make the connection between us

I felt so necessary, I was so humiliated.
I have learned not to suffer at the memory.
That recognition I wanted I had to discover in myself.
We have more in common now.

A Fable

There was a woman had a child
and loved this child's face,
a blending of two. It made her think
that there were others to combine with
to make a difference just as fine,
that she was capable of many kinds,
and she went off to have a child
with each man she loved on sight,
and in her old age, surrounded by children,
she was loved as the mother
of their understanding.

For Nobody Else

She presents me with a mountain
which to possess I first must climb.
At the start I must enter a tunnel
that winds in darkness to the top.
In my extremity, my breathing forced,
at my topmost fear as I labor,
she who has hidden her face
turns to greet the high noon burst
upon our eyes.

Lie quietly by my side
as a still lake reflecting
its mountain, my heart beats
on your heart
as we hold each other's breathing
in our arms,
our backs on darkness,
light our breaths,
safe at last
to hold you,
you to place your hands
upon my back
in the shadows.

I need to see and touch
and talk to you each day
to assure myself
I am not made happy with dreams.
Then you become for me a tree
of comforting shade, bellying
where the branches bunch together

full of leaves.
I want a maternal world.

Sadly is how I must say it
because you have many sisters
and I am brother to many brothers.
Should we then not become many happinesses,
become many starts of love,
as we fade into a crowd of faces
awaiting our bed?

My body grows pale with effort
into the milky dawn.
I succeed in acting one more day,
you already dressed and moving about,
a person with a coffee pot.
I stick out my tongue
to touch the brightening sky.

How do I know that tomorrow you will live?
Do you know how much you mean to me?
At the thought of your death
all thought stops in me,
I catch my breath.

Progress of Love

When I first met you I talked to your body,
avoided your eyes watching my next move,
to be prepared, not in hostility:
to be aware, to know my body.
I thought your eyes not human, watching;
and I was unhappy, drawn by their colorless
look, I myself suspect and your eyes a reproof,
until you spoke. Then body became an accent
of your voice. Your words delighted me,
you said simply the truth,
that with your interest each day existed,
and for that reason your body was.
Though I still love it,
that is because of you.

Marriage Song

As for life, I have not held a bouquet of roses
at your nose, nor slide scenes of the happy days.
My role has been the face machine planed,
slide slot of the lips, eyes sockets for ball bearings,
and tongue the emery stick of the motor.
You have had a city from me
who have moved through its cutting grooves,
the streets, and entered the offices and factories,
the rigid moulds, to come out beveled, shaped
and clean. Only my voice in its sharp edge
has protested; in the touch of your thought
upon me have you felt my love,
in reply cutting you. And you have wondered
for a place to keep such implement, in a house
of yielding chairs, spring mattresses and music;
and I too have wondered that somehow I had not been
returned in rack among other steel. My home,
my tool chest, does not shut out the light
or turn the key on me. I do not hang on a hook
like a hammer or nestle in a form like a plane
but stride about from room to room
to find a window from which to read
the saw-toothed buildings that cut us down to size;
and you beside me looking out. We meet here,
and I begin to soften, under a small tear
in your eye.

Oh Irene

What has happened to Irene whose bald brother
wore a wig? She asked me not to see her
and I loved her, which saddened her.
So sorry for herself, poor child,
working at Woolworth's where I would come.
She would grimace and ask me to leave.
The once she did let me walk her home after work
was to tell me of her brother's wig.
It was she felt ugly and unwanted
as she made plain she would live unhappily
because of him and did not want my love
to make her choice more difficult.
At her door, I left and slowly walked away,
ill about the wig, and unhappy for Irene
at Woolworth's where she would stand patiently
behind counter for customers. But it was not you
wearing the wig, Irene! Where are you?
Listen, I am through feeling unhappy.
I have been through for a long time!
I am grown up,
a man like your brother.

Against the Evidence

As I reach to close each book
lying open on my desk, it leaps up
to snap at my fingers. My legs
won't hold me, I must sit down.
My fingers pain me
where the thick leaves snapped together
at my touch.

         All my life
I've held books in my hands
like children, carefully turning
their pages and straightening out
their creases. I use books
almost apologetically. I believe
I often think their thoughts for them.
Reading, I never know where theirs leave off
and mine begin. I am so much alone
in the world, I can observe the stars
or study the breeze, I can count the steps
on a stair on the way up or down,
and I can look at another human being
and get a smile, knowing
it is for the sake of politeness.
Nothing must be said of estrangement
among the human race and yet
nothing is said at all
because of that.
But no book will help either.
I stroke my desk,
its wood so smooth, so patient and still.

I set a typewriter on its surface
and begin to type
to tell myself my troubles.
Against the evidence, I live by choice.

An Omen

I love the bird that appears
each day at my window.
Whether the bird loves me
I only can surmise
from its regularity.

Six Movements on a Theme

(For Denise Levertov)

Thinking myself in a warm country
of maternal trees under whose shade
I lie and doze, I dream I am weightless.
Magnified faces stare back at me—
of friends wanting me to live
to whom I am dying stretched out
on the ground and barely breathing.
Dead, they say as I hold my breath
to close in and possess myself.

I dream my life to be a plant
floating upon a quiet pool,
gathering nourishment from water
and the sun. I emerge
of my own excess power, my roots
beginning to move like legs,
my leaves like arms,
the pistil the head. I walk
out of the pool
until I reach my utmost weariness
in a dance of the fading power
of my roots—when I lie down
silently to die and find myself
afloat again.

I see no fish crawling
to become man. The mountains
have been standing
without a single effort
to transform themselves
into castles or apartment houses.
Amid silence, I set a statue
in my image.
                    I love you, man,
on my knees. To you
I will address my pleas
for help. You will save me
from myself. From your silence
I will learn to live.

I was shown my only form.
I have no hope
but to approach myself,
palm touching palm.

Tapping on a wall
I feel my humankind,
secretly content
to suffer.
I too am a wall.

The stars are burning overhead.
Excited, I understand
from a distance:
I am fire,
I'll be dumb.

An Ontology

In the dark I step out of bed
and approaching the kitchen down the foyer
run my hand over the wall, smooth and rough
by turns, with cracks, holes, lumps
and dips the whole length,
my hand forming to each.
The floor bumpy and creaking,
now straight and now sagging,
the soles of my feet shape to each change.
My shoulders compress to the narrow hallway
as they go forward with me to the kitchen,
and there my eyes blink at the light.
Because I can find no direction of my own,
I eat. I belong with the bread, the milk
and the cheese. I become their peace.
I am nourished with myself
and go back to bed. I become the mattress,
I lie upon myself, I close my eyes,
I become sleep. It rolls me over
as I dream. I become a lack of control,
happening simultaneously everywhere.
It is me, I am happening.
As I move all moves with me.
I am this all as it moves
and harm cannot come unless I happen,
but because I exist, I am existence.

Secretly

My foot awes me,
the cushion of the sole
in profile shaped like a bird's head,
the toes long and narrow like a beak,
the arch to the foot
with the gentle incline
of a bird's body
and the heel thick and stubby
like a starling's tail.
In a slow motion it ascends
and descends in a half-circle,
tense, poised for flight.
The full weight of my body
today walking on it
supporting me in my weariness
it can perform its flight,
its shape delicate, light,
swift-seeming, tense and tireless
as I lie on a bed, my foot
secretly a bird.

Gardeners

So is the child slow stooping beside him
picking radishes from the soil.
He straightens up,
his arms full of the green leaves.
She bends low to each bunch and whispers,
Please come out big and red.
Tugs at them gently to give them time to change,
if they are moody and small.
Her arms filled, she paces
beside her grandfather's elderly puppet walk.

The Life Dance

I see bubbling out of the ground:
water, fresh, a pure smell. My mind
too begins to spring. I take
small hops. I enjoy myself
partly because I have the nerve.
Is anybody watching?
I care and don't care,
as I hop, and soon
because nobody is looking I'm leaping
and twisting into awkward shapes,
letting my hands make signs
of a meaning I do not understand.
I am absorbed in getting at what
till now
I had not been aware of.

There is a feeling in the world
I sometimes think I'm grasping.
I find myself holding a hand or
as I take a deep breath
I think it is there.

Three in Transition

(For WCW)

I wish I understood the beauty
in leaves falling. To whom
are we beautiful
as we go?

I lie in the field
still, absorbing the stars
and silently throwing off
their presence. Silently
I breathe and die
by turns.

He was ripe
and fell to the ground
from a bough
out where the wind
is free
of the branches.

For My Daughter in Reply to a Question

We're not going to die,
we'll find a way.
We'll breathe deeply
and eat carefully.
We'll think always on life.
There'll be no fading for you or for me.
We'll be the first
and we'll not laugh at ourselves ever
and your children will be my grandchildren.
Nothing will have changed
except by addition.
There'll never be another as you
and never another as I.
No one ever will confuse you
nor confuse me with another.
We will not be forgotten and passed over
and buried under the births and deaths to come.

The Hope

In the woods as the trees fade in the dusk
I am unable to speak or to gesture.
I lie down to warm myself against the ground.
If I live through the night
I will be a species
related to the tree
and the cold dark.

Night at an Airport

Just as the signal tower lights flash
on and off, so the world recedes
and comes on, giving the illusion
of end and beginning. Before light
there was darkness in which the plane
kept roaring in for landing. Particles
of dust rise in the wind's path
and settle obscurely
when the wind has passed.
We have our beginnings
in breeze or storm, dancing or swirling;
and are still when the wind is still.
We have earth and return to it—
everlasting as a thought.

Anew

Dante forgot to say,
Thank you, Lord, for sending me
to hell. I find myself happier
than when I was ignorant.
I am left helpless
but more cheerful.
Nothing could be worse
than to start ignorant again.
And so I look to you
to help me love my life
anew.

Walk There

(For Marianne Moore)

The way through the woods is past trees,
touching grass, bark, stone, water and mud;
into the night of the trees, beneath
their damp cold, stumbling on roots,
discovering no trail, trudging
and smelling pine, cypress and musk.
A rabbit leaps across my path,
and something big rustles in the bush.
Stand still, eye the nearest tree
for climbing. Subside in fear
in continued silence. Walk.
See the sky splattered with leaves.
Ahead, is that too the sky
or a clearing?
Walk there.

Distinguished contemporary poetry in cloth and paperback editions

ALAN ANSEN: *Disorderly Houses* (1961)

JOHN ASHBERY: *The Tennis Court Oath* (1962)

ROBERT BAGG: *Madonna of the Cello* (1961)

ROBERT BLY: *Silence in the Snowy Fields* (1962)

TURNER CASSITY: *Watchboy, What of the Night?* (1966)

TRAM COMBS: *saint thomas. poems.* (1965)

DONALD DAVIE: *Events and Wisdoms* (1965); *New and Selected Poems* (1961)

JAMES DICKEY: *Buckdancer's Choice* (1965) [National Book Award in Poetry, 1966]; *Drowning With Others* (1962); *Helmets* (1964)

DAVID FERRY: *On the Way to the Island* (1960)

ROBERT FRANCIS: *The Orb Weaver* (1960)

JOHN HAINES: *Winter News* (1966)

RICHARD HOWARD: *The Damages* (1967); *Quantities* (1962)

BARBARA HOWES: *Light and Dark* (1959)

DAVID IGNATOW: *Figures of the Human* (1964); *Rescue the Dead* (1968); *Say Pardon* (1961)

DONALD JUSTICE: *Night Light* (1967); *The Summer Anniversaries* (1960) [A Lamont Poetry Selection]

CHESTER KALLMAN: *Absent and Present* (1963)

PHILIP LEVINE: *Not This Pig* (1968)

LOU LIPSITZ: *Cold Water* (1967)

JOSEPHINE MILES: *Kinds of Affection* (1967)

VASSAR MILLER: *My Bones Being Wiser* (1963); *Wage War on Silence* (1960)

W. R. MOSES: *Identities* (1965)

DONALD PETERSEN: *The Spectral Boy* (1964)

MARGE PIERCY: *Breaking Camp* (1968)

HYAM PLUTZIK: *Apples from Shinar* (1959)

VERN RUTSALA: *The Window* (1964)

HARVEY SHAPIRO: *Battle Report* (1966)

JON SILKIN: *Poems New and Selected* (1966)

LOUIS SIMPSON: *At the End of the Open Road* (1963) [Pulitzer Prize in Poetry, 1964]; *A Dream of Governors* (1959)

JAMES WRIGHT: *The Branch Will Not Break* (1963); *Saint Judas* (1959)